I0017152

CONTENTS

CHAPTER 1: EMBRACING CONNECTIVITY - INTRODUCTION TO STAYING CONNECTED

Connecting Hearts, Bridging Gaps

As we journey through the digital age, the ability to stay connected with our loved ones and the world around us has become more accessible than ever. For seniors, this technological landscape might seem daunting at first, but with a bit of guidance and understanding, it opens doors to a world of possibilities. This chapter is a warm invitation to embrace connectivity, emphasizing its importance in enhancing your life and well-being.

The Significance of Staying Connected

A Fountain of Youth for the Mind

Imagine having a virtual window that lets you peek into the lives of your grandchildren, share laughter with old friends, or explore the latest news from the comfort of your home. Staying connected is not just about mastering the art of technology; it's about unlocking a fountain of youth for the mind. Numerous studies have shown that active engagement with technology and social platforms can improve cognitive function, boost mood, and reduce feelings of loneliness.

The Changing Landscape of Relationships

In an era where distances can be measured in milliseconds, staying connected is no longer a luxury but a necessity. The relationships we build and maintain online are as real and significant as those we nurture in person. From virtual family reunions to heartfelt messages exchanged with friends across the globe, technology allows us to bridge gaps, fostering a sense of togetherness that transcends physical boundaries.

A Journey into the Digital World

Navigating the Digital Landscape

The digital world can be compared to a vast, bustling city. In this city, the internet serves as the main thoroughfare, connecting various neighborhoods of information, communication, and entertainment. Understanding how to navigate this city is the first step toward unlocking the potential it holds.

The Internet: More Than Just a Web

At its core, the internet is a network of interconnected computers, servers, and devices. It is the highway that facilitates the flow of information. Imagine it as a massive library where you can find answers to almost any question, connect with people from all walks of life, and explore a universe of knowledge and entertainment. This chapter will gently guide you through the basics, making the internet not just familiar but friendly.

Stories of Connection

Real-Life Tales of Seniors Embracing Technology

Before delving into the practical aspects, let's draw inspiration from real-life stories of seniors who have embraced technology with open arms. Meet Ruth, a grandmother who stays connected with her family through video calls, sharing in the joys of her grandchildren's milestones. Discover the journey of Harold, who, in his golden years, found new friends and interests through social media.

The Ripple Effect of Connectivity

These stories showcase the ripple effect of connectivity, demonstrating that it's never too late to embark on a journey of exploration and connection. The benefits extend beyond personal satisfaction to positively impact family dynamics and community engagement.

The Path Ahead

What Lies Beyond the Horizon

As we embark on this journey together, envision the path ahead not as a steep climb but as a gentle stroll with milestones of understanding and discovery. This chapter sets the stage for the chapters to come, where we'll demystify smartphones, unravel the wonders of the internet, and delve into the realm of social media. Each step will bring you closer to a world where staying connected is not just a technological feat but a joyful part of everyday life.

A Personal Pledge

Before we dive into the practicalities, take a moment to reflect on your own reasons for embracing technology. Whether it's connecting with family, exploring new hobbies, or staying updated on current events, this personal pledge will serve as your compass, guiding you through the exciting digital landscape ahead.

CHAPTER 2: NAVIGATING THE DIGITAL WATERS - UNDERSTANDING THE INTERNET

Unveiling the Internet: A Gentle Introduction

As we embark on our journey into the digital realm, understanding the basics of the internet is like learning the language of a new and exciting land. In this chapter, we'll embark on a gentle exploration, demystifying the internet and revealing its relevance in our daily lives. By the end, you'll not only be familiar with the internet's fundamental concepts but will also appreciate its role as a gateway to a world of information, communication, and entertainment.

The Internet Unveiled

A Global Network of Connections

Think of the internet as a vast, interconnected web that spans the globe. It's a network of networks, linking computers, devices, and servers worldwide. This intricate web allows information to flow seamlessly, connecting people, businesses, and ideas in real-time.

How Does It Work?

At its core, the internet operates on a simple principle: data exchange. When you request information, your device sends a signal to a server, and in return, the server provides the requested data. This back-and-forth communication happens at incredible speeds, thanks to the intricate infrastructure of cables, satellites, and data centers that make up the internet.

Navigating the Digital Landscape

Web Browsers: Your Gateway

Just as you use a car to navigate a city, you'll use a web browser to explore the internet. Popular web browsers include Chrome,

Firefox, Safari, and Edge. These browsers act as your digital vehicle, allowing you to travel from one webpage to another seamlessly.

URLs: Internet Street Addresses

Every webpage has a unique address known as a URL (Uniform Resource Locator). Think of URLs as street addresses for websites. Entering a URL into your browser's address bar is like typing in the coordinates for your destination, instantly transporting you to the desired webpage.

The Internet and You

Information Highway: Your Personal Library

Imagine the internet as a vast library where you can find information on virtually any topic. Whether you're curious about recipes, historical events, or the latest news, the internet has it all. Search engines like Google act as librarians, helping you locate the specific information you seek.

Communication Hub: Connecting with Others

Beyond information, the internet is a powerful tool for communication. Email, social media, and messaging apps enable you to connect with friends and family regardless of physical distance. We'll delve deeper into these communication tools in later chapters, but for now, recognize that the internet is not just a source of knowledge but a bridge between hearts.

Internet Basics for Seniors

Simplifying Terminology

The internet has its own vocabulary, and while some terms may sound technical, understanding them is simpler than it seems. In this section, we'll break down common terms like "browser," "URL," and "search engine" into everyday language, ensuring that you can navigate the digital landscape with ease.

Ensuring Online Safety

Just as you take precautions in the physical world, it's essential to stay vigilant online. This chapter will guide you through the basics of online safety, from recognizing secure websites to understanding the importance of strong, unique passwords. By the end, you'll feel empowered to explore the internet confidently and securely.

Stories of Internet Exploration

Real-Life Tales of Seniors Embracing the Web

To illustrate the positive impact of internet exploration, let's share stories of seniors who have embraced the digital world. Meet Clara, who discovered a passion for gardening through online forums, and James, who reconnected with old friends through social media. These stories highlight the diverse ways in which seniors can enrich their lives through internet exploration.

From Novice to Navigator

These stories showcase that the journey from internet novice to navigator is not only possible but also immensely rewarding. Whether you're seeking information, connecting with others, or exploring new hobbies, the internet is a treasure trove waiting to be discovered.

The Path Ahead

Mastering the Digital Terrain

As we conclude this chapter, envision the internet not as an intimidating wilderness but as a well-marked trail waiting for you to explore. The knowledge gained in this chapter is a compass that will guide you through future chapters, where we'll dive into the practicalities of using smartphones, engaging on social media, and harnessing the power of the internet for enriching your daily life.

A Digital Passport

Consider the knowledge gained in this chapter as your digital passport, granting you access to the vast landscape of the internet. With each click and search, you'll become more adept at navigating this digital terrain, unlocking a world of possibilities at your fingertips.

CHAPTER 3: YOUR POCKET-SIZED COMPANION - EASY-TO-USE SMARTPHONES

Navigating the Digital World with Ease

In this chapter, we'll embark on a journey into the world of smartphones - those compact marvels that fit snugly into your pocket yet hold the power to connect you with loved ones, entertain you, and open doors to the vast digital landscape. If the thought of using a smartphone seems overwhelming, fear not! We'll guide you through the essentials, making these devices not just accessible but enjoyable companions in your daily life.

The Smartphone Unveiled

More Than a Phone: A Multifunctional Device

Gone are the days when phones were merely devices for making calls. Today's smartphones are powerful computers that fit into the palm of your hand. They can take photos, play music, browse the internet, send messages, and run a myriad of applications, making them versatile companions for everyday tasks.

Touchscreen Magic: A User-Friendly Interface

One of the key features of smartphones is their touchscreen interface. No need for buttons and complicated navigation - a simple touch, swipe, or tap on the screen can accomplish a variety of actions. This chapter will guide you through the basics of using touchscreens, ensuring you feel confident navigating your smartphone.

Choosing the Right Smartphone

Simplified Options for Seniors

The market offers a variety of smartphones with different features and operating systems. Choosing the right one can seem like a daunting task, but fear not - we'll break down the options, focusing on user-friendly models and operating systems that cater specifically to seniors.

Essential Features: What to Look For

From screen size to battery life, certain features can enhance the usability of a smartphone for seniors. We'll discuss the importance of these features and guide you on what to look for when selecting your device.

Getting Started with Your Smartphone

Basic Setup: From Powering On to Home Screen

The initial setup of your smartphone can be a breeze with step-by-step guidance. We'll walk you through turning on your device, setting up your preferences, and getting acquainted with the home screen. By the end of this section, you'll feel comfortable with the basic functions of your smartphone.

Essential Apps: A Starter Kit

Smartphones come preloaded with a variety of apps, and you can download many more to suit your needs. We'll explore essential apps for communication, entertainment, and information. Whether you want to send messages, check the weather, or listen to music, we've got you covered.

Communication Made Effortless

Phone Calls and Text Messages: The Basics

Making a call or sending a text message may seem straightforward, but understanding additional features like contacts, call logs, and messaging apps can enhance your communication experience. This section will guide you through the essentials, making communication effortless.

Video Calls: Bringing Loved Ones Closer

Video calls have become a vital tool for staying connected with family and friends, especially when physical distances separate us. We'll introduce you to video calling apps, walking you through the process of making and receiving video calls. The joy of seeing your loved ones, even from afar, is just a tap away.

Tailoring Your Smartphone Experience

Accessibility Features: A Customized Experience

Smartphones come equipped with accessibility features designed to cater to diverse user needs. From adjustable text sizes to voice commands, we'll explore how you can customize your smartphone experience for maximum comfort and usability.

Personalization: Making It Yours

Your smartphone is a reflection of your preferences and personality. We'll discuss how you can personalize your device, from choosing wallpapers to organizing apps, creating a smartphone experience that feels uniquely yours.

Troubleshooting and Support

Common Issues and Solutions

Encountering challenges with your smartphone is normal, but knowing how to troubleshoot common issues can save you frustration. From dealing with frozen screens to managing storage, this section will equip you with the knowledge to resolve common problems.

Seeking Help: Support Options

If you ever find yourself in need of assistance, smartphones offer various support options. Whether it's reaching out to customer support or finding online tutorials, we'll guide you on where to seek help when needed.

Stories of Smartphone Triumphs

Real-Life Tales of Seniors Embracing Smartphones

To inspire and reassure, let's explore stories of seniors who have embraced smartphones with enthusiasm. Meet Sarah, who uses her smartphone to capture and share moments with her grandchildren, and Robert, who discovered a newfound love for audiobooks through his device. These stories showcase that, regardless of age, smartphones can become valuable tools for joy and connection.

Empowering Seniors Through Technology

These stories underscore the empowerment that comes with embracing technology. Whether it's capturing memories, discovering new interests, or staying connected with loved ones, smartphones have the potential to enhance and enrich the lives of seniors.

The Path Ahead

Mastering Your Pocket Companion

As we conclude this chapter, consider your smartphone not as a complex gadget but as a friendly companion ready to simplify your life. The knowledge gained in this chapter is your key to unlocking the full potential of your smartphone. In the upcoming chapters, we'll explore the wonders of Wi-Fi, guide you through social media platforms, and delve deeper into the world of communication technology.

A New Digital Adventure Awaits

Embrace your smartphone as a tool for connection, communication, and discovery. The path ahead is filled with exciting digital adventures, and your smartphone is the trusty guide that will lead you through each step. So, charge up your device, and get ready to explore the boundless possibilities in the palm of your hand.

CHAPTER 4: CONNECTING SEAMLESSLY - FRIENDLY WI-FI SETUP

Transforming Your Space into a Digital Haven

In this chapter, we'll unravel the world of Wi-Fi, the invisible force that connects your devices to the vast digital universe. Setting up and using Wi-Fi may seem like a complex task, but fear not - we'll guide you through the process step by step. By the end of this chapter, you'll not only be connected to the internet but will have transformed your living space into a digital haven where information, entertainment, and communication are just a click away.

Decoding the Magic of Wi-Fi

Wi-Fi Demystified

Wi-Fi, short for Wireless Fidelity, is the technology that enables devices like smartphones, laptops, and smart home gadgets to connect to the internet without the need for physical cables. It's like the invisible bridge that brings the digital world to your fingertips, allowing you to browse the web, stream videos, and communicate with loved ones effortlessly.

The Components of Wi-Fi

Understanding Wi-Fi involves recognizing its essential components. We'll introduce you to routers, the devices responsible for transmitting Wi-Fi signals, and explain how your devices, like smartphones and laptops, catch these signals to access the internet.

Preparing for Wi-Fi Setup

Choosing the Right Router

If you're setting up Wi-Fi at home, selecting the right router is crucial. We'll guide you through the process, helping you choose a router that suits your needs and living space. Factors like coverage area, speed, and compatibility with your devices will be demystified.

Wi-Fi Plans and Providers

Connecting to the internet involves choosing a Wi-Fi plan from an internet service provider (ISP). We'll walk you through the process of selecting a plan that aligns with your usage requirements, ensuring a smooth online experience without unnecessary costs.

Setting Up Wi-Fi - Step by Step

Step 1: Unboxing and Placing Your Router

The journey to Wi-Fi bliss begins with unboxing and placing your router. We'll guide you on where to position your router for optimal signal strength and coverage. Whether it's in the living room, home office, or bedroom, strategic placement is key to a reliable Wi-Fi connection.

Step 2: Connecting Your Router to Power

Once your router is in place, the next step is providing it with power. We'll guide you through the simple process of connecting your router to a power source, ensuring it's ready to broadcast Wi-Fi signals to your devices.

Step 3: Connecting Your Router to the Internet

Your router needs to be connected to the internet to provide you with Wi-Fi access. We'll walk you through connecting your router to your modem, the device that brings internet access to your home. This step is crucial for establishing a connection to the vast digital landscape.

Step 4: Configuring Wi-Fi Settings

Configuring Wi-Fi settings involves giving your Wi-Fi network a name (SSID) and setting a secure password. We'll guide you through this process, ensuring that your Wi-Fi network is not only easily identifiable but also protected from unauthorized access.

Step 5: Connecting Your Devices to Wi-Fi

With your Wi-Fi network set up, it's time to connect your devices. Whether it's a smartphone, laptop, or smart TV, we'll guide you through the process of finding and joining your Wi-Fi network. Once connected, your devices will have the power to access the internet wirelessly.

Troubleshooting Wi-Fi Issues

Common Wi-Fi Challenges

While Wi-Fi offers the convenience of wireless connectivity, it's not immune to challenges. We'll discuss common issues such as slow internet speeds, dropped connections, and dead zones. More importantly, we'll provide troubleshooting tips to overcome these challenges, ensuring a seamless online experience.

Wi-Fi Extenders and Boosters

For larger homes or areas with Wi-Fi dead zones, Wi-Fi extenders and boosters can be game-changers. We'll explore these devices, explaining how they work and guiding you on incorporating them into your home network for improved coverage.

Wi-Fi for Smart Living

Smart Home Devices and Wi-Fi

As the digital landscape evolves, smart home devices have become increasingly popular. From smart thermostats to voice-activated assistants, many of these devices rely on Wi-Fi for connectivity. We'll introduce you to the world of smart living, guiding you on incorporating these devices into your Wi-Fi network for added convenience.

Streaming and Entertainment

Wi-Fi plays a central role in streaming movies, music, and videos. We'll explore streaming services, explaining how to connect your smart TV or streaming device to Wi-Fi for a personalized and immersive entertainment experience.

Stories of Wi-Fi Triumphs

Real-Life Tales of Seniors Embracing Wi-Fi

Let's delve into stories of seniors who have embraced Wi-Fi with enthusiasm. Meet Eleanor, who connects with her book club through virtual meetings, and William, who explores the world of online cooking classes from the comfort of his kitchen. These stories showcase the transformative power of Wi-Fi in enriching daily life.

Connectivity Beyond Boundaries

These stories exemplify that Wi-Fi is not just a technological convenience but a gateway to a world of possibilities. Whether it's connecting with friends, pursuing hobbies, or accessing valuable resources, Wi-Fi empowers seniors to break through physical boundaries and embrace a connected and vibrant lifestyle.

The Path Ahead

A Connected Sanctuary

As we conclude this chapter, envision your home as a connected sanctuary where Wi-Fi weaves a digital tapestry, seamlessly integrating into your daily life. The knowledge gained in this chapter is your key to unlocking the full potential of Wi-Fi. In the upcoming chapters, we'll guide you through the world of social media, unravel the simplicity of video calls, and introduce you to the wonders of cloud services.

Embracing Connectivity with Confidence

Embrace the power of Wi-Fi with confidence, knowing that your digital sanctuary is now equipped to bring the world to your fingertips. The path ahead is filled with exciting possibilities, and with Wi-Fi as your trusty companion, you're ready to explore, connect, and thrive in the digital era.

CHAPTER 5: SOCIAL BONDS IN A DIGITAL AGE - SOCIALIZING ON SOCIAL MEDIA

A Journey into Virtual Togetherness

In this chapter, we'll explore the vibrant world of social media, where connections transcend physical boundaries, and friendships find new dimensions. Social media platforms provide a space for sharing, caring, and staying connected with loved ones. If the idea of navigating these digital landscapes seems overwhelming, fear not - we'll guide you through the process with ease, ensuring that socializing on social media becomes a joyful and enriching part of your digital journey.

The Essence of Social Media

Beyond Likes and Shares

Social media platforms are more than just spaces for posting updates and sharing photos; they are digital communities that foster connections. Whether it's rekindling old friendships, staying updated on family news, or discovering shared interests, social media has the power to bring people together in meaningful ways.

Understanding Different Platforms

There's a diverse array of social media platforms, each with its unique features and purposes. From the visual allure of Instagram to the conversational landscape of Facebook and the professional networking on LinkedIn, we'll guide you through popular platforms and help you choose the ones that align with your preferences.

Creating Your Social Media Presence

Setting Up Your Profile

Your social media profile is your digital identity. We'll walk you through the process of creating a profile, from choosing a profile picture to writing a bio that reflects your personality. This step is crucial for making a positive impression and connecting with others who share your interests.

Navigating Privacy Settings

Understanding and managing privacy settings is essential for a secure and comfortable social media experience. We'll guide you through the settings, helping you control who sees your posts, who can connect with you, and what information is visible on your profile.

Connecting with Friends and Family

Finding and Adding Friends

One of the joys of social media is reconnecting with friends and family. We'll show you how to find and add friends, whether they are nearby or miles away. Rekindling connections from the past and staying updated on the present becomes a seamless experience.

Sharing Updates and Moments

Sharing updates, photos, and moments is at the heart of social media. We'll guide you through the process of creating and sharing posts, ensuring that your social media presence reflects the richness of your life. From family gatherings to personal achievements, your digital journey becomes a canvas for sharing joy.

Exploring Interests and Communities

Joining Groups and Pages

Social media offers a multitude of groups and pages dedicated to various interests. Whether it's gardening, book clubs, or travel enthusiasts, we'll guide you through joining and engaging with communities that align with your passions. Discovering like-minded individuals becomes a delightful journey of exploration.

Engaging with Content

Liking, commenting, and sharing content are ways to engage with others on social media. We'll provide tips on how to interact with posts and contribute meaningfully to conversations. Engaging with content fosters a sense of virtual togetherness and creates a supportive digital community.

Staying Safe on Social Media

Recognizing and Avoiding Scams

While social media is a space for connection, it's essential to stay vigilant against scams. We'll discuss common social media scams and provide guidance on recognizing and avoiding them. Your safety in the digital world is a priority, and we'll equip you with the knowledge to navigate social media securely.

Unplugging When Needed

Finding balance in your digital life is crucial for well-being. We'll discuss the importance of setting boundaries, managing screen time, and knowing when to unplug. Social media is a tool for connection, not an obligation, and we'll guide you on navigating it in a way that enhances rather than overwhelms your life.

Stories of Social Media Joys

Real-Life Tales of Seniors Embracing Social Media

Let's explore stories of seniors who have embraced social media with enthusiasm. Meet Margaret, who reconnects with childhood friends through Facebook, and George, who shares his photography passion on Instagram. These stories showcase the diverse ways social media can bring joy, connection, and new opportunities into your life.

A Tapestry of Digital Connections

These stories exemplify that social media is not just a digital space but a vibrant tapestry of connections waiting to be woven. Whether it's forging new friendships, exploring shared interests, or staying updated on family milestones, social media becomes a canvas for a rich and fulfilling digital life.

The Path Ahead

Embracing the Digital Tapestry

As we conclude this chapter, envision social media not as a virtual distraction but as a tapestry where your digital connections and experiences create a beautiful mosaic. The knowledge gained in this chapter is your key to navigating social media with confidence. In the upcoming chapters, we'll unravel the simplicity of video calls, explore the wonders of cloud services, and guide you through the basics of email communication.

Digital Togetherness Awaits

Embrace the world of social media with open arms, knowing that it's a space where connections flourish, and friendships find new dimensions. The path ahead is filled with opportunities to explore, share, and connect. With social media as your virtual playground, you're ready to dive into the joy of digital togetherness.

CHAPTER 6: EMBRACING FACE-TO-FACE IN A DIGITAL WORLD - VIDEO CALLS MADE SIMPLE

Bridging Distances with Virtual Presence

In this chapter, we'll embark on a journey into the world of video calls, where faces light up screens, and voices traverse the digital landscape. Video calls offer a unique way to connect with loved ones, fostering a sense of closeness even when miles apart. If the idea of video calls seems daunting, fear not - we'll guide you through the process step by step, ensuring that video calls become a source of joy and connection in your digital repertoire.

The Essence of Video Calls

Beyond Words: A Visual Connection

Video calls go beyond traditional phone conversations by adding a visual dimension to communication. Whether it's seeing the smiles of grandchildren, sharing a virtual cup of tea with friends, or attending a family celebration from afar, video calls bridge the gap between physical distances, creating a sense of virtual togetherness.

The Rise of Video Communication

With the advent of smartphones, tablets, and computers equipped with cameras, video communication has become more accessible than ever. Platforms like Zoom, Skype, and FaceTime bring loved ones face-to-face, transforming conversations into shared experiences.

Choosing the Right Platform

Zoom, Skype, FaceTime, and More

Different platforms cater to various needs and preferences. We'll guide you through popular video call platforms, explaining their features and helping you choose the one that aligns with your device and the preferences of those you wish to connect with.

Setting Up Your Account

Creating an account on a video call platform is the first step to virtual face-to-face conversations. We'll walk you through the account setup process, ensuring that you're ready to embark on the exciting journey of video calls with confidence.

Initiating and Receiving Video Calls

Making Your First Call

Initiating a video call may feel like a leap into the unknown, but we'll guide you through the process. From selecting contacts to hitting the call button, making your first video call will be a breeze. We'll also cover the etiquette of sending and receiving calls, ensuring smooth virtual interactions.

Exploring Call Features

Video call platforms offer features beyond just seeing and hearing each other. We'll delve into functions like screen sharing, virtual backgrounds, and chat options, enhancing your video call experience and making each conversation uniquely enjoyable.

Staying Connected on Different Devices

Smartphones, Tablets, and Computers

Video calls are not limited to a specific device; you can connect with loved ones using smartphones, tablets, or computers. We'll guide you on making video calls on various devices, ensuring that you can choose the platform and device that best suits your preferences.

Connecting with Smart TVs

For a larger-than-life video call experience, connecting with smart TVs is a fantastic option. We'll explore how to use platforms like Zoom on smart TVs, turning your living room into a virtual meeting space for family gatherings or catching up with friends.

Troubleshooting Video Call Hiccups

Common Issues and Solutions

While video calls are generally smooth, technical glitches can occasionally occur. We'll provide troubleshooting tips for common issues like poor video quality, audio problems, or difficulty connecting. Your virtual journey should be free of obstacles, and we're here to guide you past any hiccups.

Practice Makes Perfect

Feeling apprehensive about video calls is entirely normal. We'll encourage you to practice with a friend or family member, allowing you to become more comfortable with the platform and features. The more you engage in video calls, the more natural and enjoyable they become.

Etiquette and Best Practices

Virtual Etiquette

Just like in-person interactions, virtual conversations have their own set of etiquettes. We'll discuss best practices for video calls, from finding the right camera angle to minimizing background noise. Following these etiquettes enhances the overall experience for both you and your virtual companions.

Planning Virtual Gatherings

For special occasions or family reunions, planning virtual gatherings can be a delightful experience. We'll guide you on coordinating group calls, scheduling events, and ensuring that everyone feels included in the virtual celebration.

Stories of Virtual Hugs

Real-Life Tales of Seniors Embracing Video Calls

Let's explore stories of seniors who have embraced video calls with enthusiasm. Meet Emily, who celebrates birthdays with her grandchildren through FaceTime, and Charles, who attends virtual book club meetings with friends. These stories illustrate the warmth and joy that video calls bring to the lives of seniors.

The Power of Visual Connection

These stories exemplify that video calls are not just a technological tool but a conduit for virtual hugs, laughter, and shared moments. Whether it's connecting with family, participating in group activities, or attending virtual events, video calls become a cherished aspect of a connected and vibrant life.

The Path Ahead

A Window to Virtual Togetherness

As we conclude this chapter, envision video calls not as a complex technology but as a virtual window connecting you to the faces and voices of loved ones. The knowledge gained in this chapter is your key to unlocking the full potential of video calls. In the upcoming chapters, we'll delve into the simplicity of cloud services, explore the basics of email communication, and introduce you to the wonders of smart home devices.

A Digital World Awaits

Embrace video calls as a means to stay visually connected with loved ones, knowing that each call is a virtual hug that transcends physical distances. The path ahead is filled with opportunities to share, laugh, and connect. With video calls as your digital bridge, you're ready to embark on a journey of virtual togetherness.

CHAPTER 7: BEYOND THE CLOUDS - CLOUD SERVICES WITHOUT CONFUSION

Unlocking the Power of Digital Storage and Accessibility

In this chapter, we'll explore the concept of cloud services - the virtual space where your digital world expands beyond the confines of your device. Cloud services offer a seamless way to store, access, and share photos, documents, and more across multiple devices. If the cloud seems like a mysterious entity, worry not - we'll demystify it and guide you through the process, ensuring that cloud services become a tool for organized and accessible digital living.

The Magic of the Cloud

A Digital Extension of Your Space

Think of the cloud as a virtual extension of your device's storage. It's a secure and scalable space where you can store files, photos, and documents, freeing up storage on your device and ensuring that your digital life is accessible from anywhere with an internet connection.

Cloud Services in Everyday Life

From saving photos on your smartphone to collaborating on documents with colleagues, cloud services are an integral part of everyday life. We'll explore how cloud services simplify tasks, enhance collaboration, and provide a secure backup for your valuable digital assets.

Understanding How the Cloud Works

Cloud Storage vs. Local Storage

Understanding the difference between cloud storage and local storage is fundamental. Local storage resides on your device, while cloud storage is hosted on remote servers accessible via the internet. We'll demystify these concepts, showcasing the advantages of cloud storage for accessibility and collaboration.

Uploading and Syncing

Uploading files to the cloud involves transferring them from your device to remote servers. Syncing ensures that changes made on one device are reflected across all connected devices. We'll guide you through the process of uploading and syncing files, making the cloud a seamless extension of your digital space.

Choosing the Right Cloud Service

Popular Cloud Service Providers

There are various cloud service providers, each offering unique features and storage plans. We'll explore popular options like Google Drive, Dropbox, and iCloud, helping you choose the one that aligns with your device preferences and storage needs.

Setting Up Your Cloud Account

Creating a cloud account is the first step to harnessing the power of cloud services. We'll walk you through the account setup process, ensuring that you're ready to explore the convenience and accessibility that cloud storage offers.

Navigating Cloud Services

Organizing Your Digital Space

Once your cloud account is set up, organizing your digital space becomes essential. We'll guide you through creating folders, naming conventions, and organizing files to ensure that your cloud storage is not only functional but also easy to navigate.

Sharing and Collaborating

One of the significant advantages of cloud services is the ability to share and collaborate on files. Whether it's a family photo album or a work document, we'll explore how to share files securely and collaborate with others in real-time.

Security and Privacy in the Cloud

Understanding Security Measures

Security is a top priority when it comes to the cloud. We'll discuss encryption, two-factor authentication, and other security measures implemented by cloud service providers to safeguard your data. Understanding these features ensures a secure digital environment.

Privacy Considerations

While cloud services offer convenience, it's essential to be mindful of privacy. We'll discuss privacy considerations, including adjusting sharing settings, being aware of terms of service, and ensuring that your data is handled responsibly by the cloud service provider.

Accessing the Cloud on Different Devices

Smartphones, Tablets, and Computers

Cloud services provide a seamless experience across various devices. We'll guide you on accessing your cloud storage from smartphones, tablets, and computers, ensuring that your files are within reach, no matter which device you're using.

Offline Access

In situations where an internet connection is unavailable, offline access to cloud-stored files becomes crucial. We'll explore how to enable offline access and work on files even when not connected to the internet.

Troubleshooting Cloud Challenges

Common Issues and Solutions

While cloud services are generally reliable, you might encounter occasional challenges. We'll provide troubleshooting tips for common issues like syncing errors, file access problems, and other hiccups that may arise. Your journey in the cloud should be smooth, and we're here to guide you past any obstacles.

Regular Maintenance

Maintaining your cloud storage involves periodic housekeeping tasks. We'll discuss archiving, deleting unnecessary files, and keeping your digital space organized. Regular maintenance ensures that your cloud storage remains efficient and clutter-free.

Stories of Cloud Triumphs

Real-Life Tales of Seniors Embracing Cloud Services

Let's explore stories of seniors who have embraced cloud services with enthusiasm. Meet Richard, who shares travel photos with family members through Google Drive, and Grace, who collaborates on family recipes using Dropbox. These stories illustrate the practical and meaningful ways cloud services enhance the lives of seniors.

A Digital Haven in the Cloud

These stories exemplify that the cloud is not just a storage solution but a digital haven where memories, documents, and experiences are securely stored and easily accessible. Whether it's sharing moments with loved ones or collaborating on creative projects, cloud services become an integral part of a connected and organized life.

The Path Ahead

A Digital Space without Boundaries

As we conclude this chapter, envision the cloud not as a distant entity but as an extension of your digital space, seamlessly connecting your devices and simplifying your digital life. The knowledge gained in this chapter is your key to unlocking the full potential of cloud services. In the upcoming chapters, we'll guide you through the basics of email communication, introduce

CHAPTER 8: CRAFTING YOUR DIGITAL LETTERS - EMAIL FOR SENIORS

Navigating the World of Electronic Communication

In this chapter, we'll delve into the realm of email communication, a digital avenue where words become letters and messages transcend physical distances. Email serves as a powerful tool for staying connected, sharing thoughts, and keeping up with the world. If the world of email seems overwhelming, fret not - we'll guide you through the process, making electronic communication a seamless and enjoyable part of your digital journey.

The Significance of Email

Beyond Traditional Letters

Email is the modern-day equivalent of handwritten letters, allowing you to communicate instantly with loved ones, friends, and even colleagues. It's a versatile tool for sharing news, sending photos, and staying updated on various aspects of life.

Importance of Digital Communication

In an era where digital communication is prevalent, email stands out as a reliable and universal method. Whether it's personal or professional, email bridges the gap between physical distances and enables timely and efficient communication.

Understanding the Basics of Email

Email Accounts and Addresses

Creating an email account is the first step to entering the world of electronic communication. We'll guide you through the process of setting up an email account, explaining the components of an email address and how to choose one that suits you.

Navigating the Email Interface

Once your email account is set up, understanding the email

interface becomes crucial. We'll walk you through the elements of an email, from the inbox to the compose window, ensuring that you feel confident navigating your email platform.

Choosing the Right Email Service

Popular Email Platforms

There are various email service providers, each offering unique features and interfaces. We'll explore popular options like Gmail, Yahoo Mail, and Outlook, helping you choose the platform that aligns with your preferences and needs.

Customizing Email Settings

Customizing your email settings enhances your user experience. We'll guide you through adjusting settings like notifications, display preferences, and signature options, making your email platform a personalized and efficient space.

Sending and Receiving Emails

Composing Emails

Composing an email involves more than just typing a message. We'll explore the elements of a well-crafted email, from addressing recipients to attaching files and adding a touch of personalization. Crafting emails becomes an art that reflects your communication style.

Receiving and Managing Emails

As emails flow into your inbox, managing them efficiently becomes essential. We'll discuss techniques for organizing emails, creating folders, and utilizing features like filters and labels. Keeping your inbox tidy ensures that important messages are easily accessible.

Advanced Email Features

Attachments and Multimedia

Emails are not limited to text; you can attach photos, documents, and multimedia files. We'll guide you through the process of attaching files to your emails, making it easy to share memories and important documents.

Email Signatures and Labels

Email signatures add a professional touch to your messages, while labels help organize your emails systematically. We'll explore how to create and customize email signatures, as well as how to use labels for efficient email categorization.

Staying Safe in the Email World

Recognizing Email Scams

Email scams are prevalent, and it's crucial to be vigilant. We'll discuss common email scams, such as phishing and fraudulent messages, and provide guidance on recognizing and avoiding them. Your email safety is a priority, and we'll equip you with the knowledge to navigate your inbox securely.

Privacy and Security Measures

Email providers implement security features to protect your account. We'll discuss measures like two-factor authentication, secure connections, and regular password updates to ensure that your email communication remains private and secure.

Email Etiquette

Crafting Polite and Effective Emails

Just as in traditional communication, email has its own set of etiquettes. We'll discuss best practices for writing polite and effective emails, from choosing appropriate language to structuring your messages for clarity. Following email etiquette enhances your communication and fosters positive interactions.

Responding Promptly

Timely responses are key to effective email communication. We'll discuss strategies for managing your inbox, prioritizing messages, and responding promptly, ensuring that your email interactions are efficient and respectful of others' time.

Stories of Email Connections

Real-Life Tales of Seniors Embracing Email

Let's explore stories of seniors who have embraced email with enthusiasm. Meet Elizabeth, who connects with her grandchildren through regular email updates, and James, who uses email for keeping in touch with friends from around the world. These stories illustrate the meaningful connections that email can foster in the lives of seniors.

A Written Symphony of Connections

These stories exemplify that email is not just a tool for digital communication but a medium through which relationships are nurtured and stories are shared. Whether it's bridging generational gaps or connecting across borders, email becomes a symphony of written connections.

The Path Ahead

A Digital Quill at Your Fingertips

As we conclude this chapter, envision email not as a complex technology but as a digital quill that allows you to craft messages, share news, and stay connected with the world. The knowledge gained in this chapter is your key to unlocking the full potential of email communication. In the upcoming chapters, we'll introduce you to the wonders of smart home devices, explore the essentials of staying safe online, and take an optimistic peek into upcoming technologies that can further enhance your digital journey.

A World of Words Awaits

Embrace the world of email with open arms, knowing that each message sent is a thread woven into the tapestry of your digital connections. The path ahead is filled with opportunities to express, share, and connect. With email as your digital quill, you're ready to embark on a journey of written connections in the digital age.

CHAPTER 9: NAVIGATING THE DIGITAL WORKPLACE - STAY CONNECTED WHILE WORKING FROM HOME

A Guide to Remote Productivity for Seniors

In this chapter, we'll explore the world of remote work, offering insights and practical tips for seniors who wish to stay connected and productive from the comfort of their homes. Working remotely has become increasingly common, and with the right tools and mindset, seniors can seamlessly adapt to the digital workplace. If the idea of working from home seems daunting, fear not - we'll guide you through the process, ensuring that your home becomes a productive and connected workspace.

The Changing Landscape of Work

The Rise of Remote Work

Over the past few years, remote work has evolved from a niche concept to a mainstream way of conducting business. The flexibility and convenience it offers have become particularly relevant, allowing individuals, including seniors, to contribute to the workforce from the comfort of their homes.

Adapting to a Digital Work Environment

The digital workplace is characterized by virtual meetings, collaborative tools, and cloud-based productivity platforms. We'll explore how seniors can adapt to this environment, showcasing the accessibility and benefits of remote work.

Setting Up Your Home Workspace

Creating a Productive Environment

Designing a home workspace is crucial for remote productivity. We'll guide you through the process of choosing a suitable location, arranging furniture, and ensuring that your home workspace is conducive to focus and efficiency.

Essential Equipment and Tools

Equipping your home workspace with the right tools is essential. We'll discuss the importance of a reliable computer, a comfortable chair, and other accessories that contribute to an ergonomic and effective home office setup.

Connecting to Virtual Meetings

Embracing Video Conferencing

Virtual meetings have become the norm in remote work scenarios. We'll explore popular video conferencing platforms like Zoom and Microsoft Teams, guiding you through the process of joining, hosting, and participating in virtual meetings.

Troubleshooting Virtual Meeting Challenges

While virtual meetings are convenient, technical challenges can arise. We'll provide troubleshooting tips for common issues such as audio or video problems, ensuring that you can navigate virtual meetings smoothly.

Collaborative Tools for Remote Work

Cloud-Based Productivity Platforms

Collaborative tools like Google Workspace and Microsoft 365 offer a suite of applications for document creation, editing, and sharing. We'll explore these platforms, demonstrating how they facilitate seamless collaboration and communication in a remote work setting.

Project Management Tools

For those engaged in projects or tasks, project management tools like Trello or Asana can enhance organization and efficiency. We'll guide you on incorporating these tools into your remote work routine for streamlined project coordination.

Time Management and Productivity

Establishing a Routine

Maintaining a routine is essential for remote productivity. We'll discuss strategies for setting a daily schedule, establishing work hours, and creating a sense of structure in your remote work routine.

Avoiding Distractions

Working from home can come with its own set of distractions. We'll provide tips on minimizing disruptions, setting boundaries, and creating a focused work environment that allows you to be productive.

Staying Connected with Colleagues

Virtual Watercooler Moments

Building and maintaining connections with colleagues is crucial for a positive remote work experience. We'll explore the concept of virtual watercooler moments, discussing ways to engage with coworkers informally and foster a sense of camaraderie.

Networking in the Digital Age

Networking remains relevant in a digital work environment. We'll guide you on leveraging professional networking platforms and participating in virtual events to expand your professional connections and opportunities.

Balancing Work and Personal Life

Setting Boundaries

Maintaining a healthy work-life balance is essential. We'll discuss the importance of setting boundaries, both in terms of time and space, to ensure that work responsibilities do not encroach on personal time.

Taking Breaks and Practicing Self-Care

Taking breaks and practicing self-care are crucial for overall well-being. We'll provide suggestions for incorporating short breaks, relaxation techniques, and self-care practices into your remote work routine.

Navigating Digital Work Challenges

Overcoming Technological Hurdles

Technological challenges can be a part of remote work. We'll offer solutions to common issues like software glitches, internet connectivity problems, and other technological hurdles that may arise.

Coping with Isolation

Remote work can sometimes lead to feelings of isolation. We'll discuss strategies for staying connected with friends, family, and colleagues, ensuring that you maintain a sense of community even while working remotely.

Stories of Remote Work Triumphs

Real-Life Tales of Seniors Embracing Remote Work

Let's explore stories of seniors who have embraced remote work with enthusiasm. Meet Susan, who runs her consulting business from home, and Robert, who participates in virtual volunteer opportunities. These stories illustrate the diverse ways seniors can thrive in the digital workplace.

A Symphony of Remote Productivity

These stories exemplify that remote work is not just a trend but a transformative way for seniors to contribute their skills, pursue passions, and stay engaged in meaningful activities from the comfort of their homes.

The Path Ahead

A Productive Haven in Your Home

As we conclude this chapter, envision your home not just as a place of residence but as a productive haven where you can contribute to work and activities that matter. The knowledge gained in this chapter is your key to unlocking the full potential of remote work. In the upcoming chapters, we'll explore the wonders of senior-friendly smart home devices, discuss practical tips for staying safe online, and take an optimistic look at upcoming technologies that can further enhance your digital journey.

Embracing Remote Productivity

Embrace the world of remote work with open arms, knowing that your skills, experiences, and contributions are valuable in the digital landscape. The path ahead is filled with opportunities to work, connect, and thrive. With the digital workplace as your canvas, you're ready to embark on a journey of remote productivity.

CHAPTER 10: ENHANCING YOUR LIVING SPACE - SENIOR-FRIENDLY SMART HOME DEVICES

A Guide to Technological Comfort and Convenience

In this chapter, we'll explore the world of smart home devices designed with seniors in mind, transforming living spaces into intuitive and responsive environments. From smart lighting to voice-activated assistants, these devices aim to enhance comfort, safety, and overall well-being. If the idea of integrating technology into your home seems complex, fear not - we'll guide you through the process, ensuring that smart home devices become valuable companions in your daily life.

The Evolution of Smart Homes

From Sci-Fi to Reality

The concept of smart homes, once confined to science fiction, has become a reality. Today, smart home devices offer a range of features designed to simplify tasks, improve accessibility, and create a more comfortable living environment.

Benefits for Seniors

Smart home devices cater to the specific needs of seniors, providing solutions that enhance safety, independence, and overall quality of life. We'll explore how these technologies can be seamlessly integrated into your living space, offering both convenience and peace of mind.

Creating a Smart Home Ecosystem

Understanding Connectivity

Smart home devices operate within an interconnected ecosystem. We'll delve into the concept of connectivity, discussing how devices communicate with each other and how they can be controlled through a central hub or a smartphone app.

Compatibility and Integration

Ensuring compatibility among your smart home devices is key to a seamless experience. We'll guide you through choosing devices that work well together and integrating them into your home ecosystem for a cohesive and efficient setup.

Essential Senior-Friendly Smart Home Devices

Smart Lighting

Adjusting lighting to suit different needs is made easy with smart lighting systems. We'll explore devices that allow you to control brightness, color, and schedules, promoting a well-lit and comfortable living space.

Smart Thermostats

Maintaining a comfortable temperature in your home becomes effortless with smart thermostats. We'll discuss devices that adapt to your preferences, optimize energy efficiency, and can be controlled remotely.

Voice-Activated Assistants

Voice-activated assistants, such as Amazon's Alexa and Google Assistant, provide hands-free control over various devices. We'll explore how these assistants can be used to set reminders, ask questions, and control other smart devices in your home.

Smart Security Systems

Enhancing home security is a priority, and smart security systems offer advanced features. We'll discuss devices such as smart doorbells, cameras, and door/window sensors that contribute to a secure living environment.

Smart Plugs and Outlets

Transforming traditional appliances into smart devices is made possible with smart plugs and outlets. We'll explore how these devices enable you to control and monitor electrical devices remotely, promoting energy efficiency and convenience.

Smart Sensors for Health Monitoring

Smart sensors can be utilized for health monitoring, providing insights into daily activities and well-being. We'll discuss devices that track movement, sleep patterns, and other health metrics, promoting proactive health management.

Smart Medication Dispensers

Managing medications becomes easier with smart medication dispensers. We'll explore devices that provide reminders, dispense the correct dosage, and send notifications to caregivers, ensuring medication adherence.

Smart Home Hubs

Centralized control of smart home devices is facilitated through smart home hubs. We'll discuss how these hubs serve as command centers, allowing you to manage multiple devices through a single interface.

Setting Up and Using Smart Home Devices

Installation and Configuration

Installing smart home devices is generally user-friendly, but guidance can be helpful. We'll provide step-by-step instructions for setting up devices, connecting them to your home network, and configuring settings to suit your preferences.

Voice Commands and Control

Using voice-activated assistants involves learning specific commands and controls. We'll provide a list of common voice commands for tasks like adjusting thermostat settings, turning lights on/off, and asking for information.

Addressing Concerns and Ensuring Safety

Privacy and Security Considerations

As with any technology, privacy and security are paramount. We'll discuss best practices for securing your smart home devices, including setting strong passwords, updating firmware, and understanding data privacy policies.

Safeguarding Against Cybersecurity Threats

Smart home devices are susceptible to cybersecurity threats. We'll provide tips on safeguarding your devices against potential breaches and ensuring that your smart home ecosystem remains secure.

Stories of Smart Home Transformations

Real-Life Tales of Seniors Embracing Smart Home Devices

Let's explore stories of seniors who have embraced smart home devices with enthusiasm. Meet Margaret, who uses smart lighting for creating a cozy ambiance, and Richard, who relies on a smart security system for peace of mind. These stories illustrate the transformative impact of smart home technologies in the lives of seniors.

A Symphony of Technological Comfort

These stories exemplify that smart home devices are not just gadgets but contributors to a symphony of comfort, convenience, and enhanced living. Whether it's improving safety, simplifying daily tasks, or promoting well-being, smart home technologies become indispensable companions in the lives of seniors.

The Path Ahead

Embracing Smart Living

As we conclude this chapter, envision your home not just as a physical space but as a smart living environment designed to cater to your needs. The knowledge gained in this chapter is your key to unlocking the full potential of senior-friendly smart home devices. In the upcoming chapters, we'll explore practical tips for staying safe online, discuss the importance of cybersecurity, and take an optimistic look at upcoming technologies that can further enhance your digital journey.

A Smart Haven Awaits

Embrace the world of smart home devices with open arms, knowing that each device is a step towards a more comfortable, convenient, and connected living space. The path ahead is filled with opportunities to enhance your daily life. With smart home technologies as your companions, you're ready to embark on a journey of technological comfort and convenience.

CHAPTER 11: NAVIGATING THE CYBER SEAS - STAYING SAFE ONLINE

A Comprehensive Guide to Digital Security for Seniors

In this chapter, we'll embark on a journey into the realm of online safety, providing seniors with essential knowledge and practical tips to navigate the digital landscape securely. As the internet becomes an integral part of daily life, understanding how to protect yourself online is crucial. If the digital world feels like uncharted waters, fear not - we'll guide you through the process, ensuring that your online experiences are safe, enjoyable, and empowering.

The Importance of Online Safety

The Digital Age Landscape

In the digital age, the internet offers countless opportunities for learning, communication, and entertainment. However, it's essential to be aware of potential risks and adopt practices that safeguard your personal information and digital well-being.

Empowerment Through Knowledge

Understanding the fundamentals of online safety empowers you to explore the vast digital landscape confidently. We'll explore practical strategies to help you stay safe while enjoying the benefits of the internet.

Building a Foundation of Online Security

Password Management

Strong and unique passwords form the first line of defense against unauthorized access. We'll discuss strategies for creating secure passwords, managing them effectively, and utilizing password manager tools to enhance security.

Two-Factor Authentication

Adding an extra layer of security through two-factor authentication strengthens your online accounts. We'll guide you on enabling and using two-factor authentication to protect your accounts from unauthorized access.

Recognizing and Avoiding Online Threats

Identifying Phishing Attempts

Phishing attempts, where attackers try to deceive you into revealing sensitive information, are prevalent. We'll discuss common signs of phishing emails and provide tips on how to recognize and avoid falling victim to these scams.

Malware Protection

Protecting your devices from malware is essential for a secure online experience. We'll explore antivirus software, anti-malware tools, and safe browsing practices to minimize the risk of malware infections.

Safe Online Shopping and Banking

Secure Transactions

Online shopping and banking have become commonplace, requiring heightened security measures. We'll discuss tips for secure online transactions, including using trusted websites, checking for secure connections, and monitoring account activity.

Avoiding Scams and Frauds

As online platforms grow, so do scams and fraudulent activities. We'll provide guidance on recognizing and avoiding common online scams, protecting your financial information from exploitation.

Social Media Safety

Privacy Settings and Controls

Social media platforms offer connectivity but also pose privacy risks. We'll guide you through adjusting privacy settings, controlling who sees your information, and navigating social media safely.

Recognizing and Avoiding Social Engineering

Social engineering tactics involve manipulating individuals to divulge confidential information. We'll discuss common social engineering techniques and provide tips on safeguarding your personal information.

Digital Footprint Management

Understanding Your Digital Footprint

Every online action contributes to your digital footprint. We'll explore the concept of a digital footprint, discuss its implications, and provide tips for managing and minimizing your online presence.

Reputation and Image Protection

Your online reputation is valuable. We'll guide you on steps to protect your reputation, address online misinformation, and maintain a positive digital image.

Educating Yourself and Others

Staying Informed

The digital landscape evolves, and staying informed about emerging threats and security best practices is crucial. We'll discuss reputable sources for online safety information and strategies for staying updated.

Educating Family and Friends

Sharing knowledge about online safety with family and friends is a collective effort. We'll explore ways to educate your social circles, promoting a safer online environment for everyone.

Online Safety for Seniors: Real-Life Scenarios

Case Studies of Cybersecurity Challenges

Let's explore real-life scenarios where seniors encountered online security challenges and successfully navigated them. These case studies provide insights into practical strategies and highlight the resilience of seniors in the digital realm.

Digital Resilience and Adaptability

These case studies exemplify that with knowledge and adaptability, seniors can overcome online security challenges, showcasing digital resilience and an ability to thrive in the ever-changing digital landscape.

The Path Ahead

A Secure Digital Horizon

As we conclude this chapter, envision the digital world not as a treacherous sea but as a horizon of opportunities where your safety is a priority. The knowledge gained in this chapter is your key to unlocking the full potential of online safety. In the upcoming chapters, we'll take an optimistic look at upcoming technologies that can further enhance your digital journey and explore the possibilities of tomorrow's technology.

Navigating Cyber Seas with Confidence

Navigate the cyber seas with confidence, knowing that your understanding of online safety equips you to explore the digital landscape securely. The path ahead is filled with opportunities to connect, learn, and enjoy the digital world responsibly. With online safety as your compass, you're ready to embark on a journey of secure and empowered digital experiences.

CHAPTER 12: EMBRACING TOMORROW - EXPLORING FUTURE TECHNOLOGIES FOR SENIORS

A Glimpse into the Technological Horizons

In this chapter, we'll embark on an optimistic exploration of future technologies that hold the potential to further enhance the lives of seniors. As technology continues to advance, new innovations emerge, offering exciting possibilities for connectivity, healthcare, and overall well-being. If the future of technology seems like a distant landscape, fear not - we'll guide you through the potential developments and their impact on the lives of seniors.

The Ever-Advancing Technological Landscape

Technological Acceleration

The pace of technological advancement continues to accelerate, bringing forth innovations that redefine how we live, work, and connect. We'll discuss the broader technological trends that are shaping the future and their potential impact on the lives of seniors.

Tailoring Innovations for Seniors

As technology evolves, there is an increasing focus on creating solutions that cater specifically to the needs and preferences of seniors. We'll explore how future technologies aim to enhance accessibility, promote well-being, and provide new avenues for connection.

Connectivity Beyond Boundaries

5G Technology

The fifth generation of wireless technology, 5G, promises ultra-fast connectivity with low latency. We'll explore how 5G can revolutionize internet speeds, making online activities, from video calls to streaming, more seamless and enjoyable.

Internet of Things (IoT) Integration

The Internet of Things (IoT) involves connecting everyday devices to the internet, creating a network of interconnected systems. We'll discuss how IoT integration can lead to smart homes that respond intuitively to seniors' needs, enhancing comfort and efficiency.

Personalized Healthcare Technologies

Remote Health Monitoring

Advancements in remote health monitoring technologies offer the potential for seniors to manage their health from the comfort of their homes. We'll explore wearable devices, smart sensors, and other innovations that enable real-time health tracking and communication with healthcare professionals.

AI-Powered Healthcare Assistance

Artificial Intelligence (AI) is poised to play a significant role in personalized healthcare. We'll discuss how AI can assist in diagnosing medical conditions, providing medication reminders, and offering virtual healthcare consultations.

Assisted Living Technologies

Robot Companions

The integration of robotics into daily life is on the horizon. We'll explore the concept of robot companions designed to assist with daily tasks, provide companionship, and enhance the overall well-being of seniors.

Smart Home Evolution

The future of smart homes involves more intuitive and responsive technologies. We'll discuss advancements in smart home devices, from voice-activated assistants to automated home management systems, that create environments tailored to seniors' preferences.

Virtual Reality (VR) and Augmented Reality (AR)

Immersive Experiences

Virtual and augmented reality technologies offer immersive experiences that can benefit seniors in various ways. We'll explore applications such as virtual travel, therapy, and interactive learning that can enhance the quality of life for seniors.

Augmented Reality in Daily Tasks

Augmented reality has the potential to assist seniors in daily tasks by overlaying digital information onto the physical world. We'll discuss how AR glasses and applications can provide guidance, translation, and contextual information in real-time.

Mind-Body Wellness Technologies

Brain-Computer Interfaces

Advancements in brain-computer interfaces hold promise for seniors in maintaining cognitive health. We'll explore how these interfaces can enable communication, control devices, and potentially aid in neurorehabilitation.

Wearable Stress and Wellness Trackers

Wearable devices designed to track stress levels and overall wellness can provide valuable insights into mental and physical health. We'll discuss how these trackers can empower seniors to proactively manage their well-being.

Sustainable and Eco-Friendly Technologies

Green Technologies

The future of technology is intertwined with sustainability. We'll explore green technologies that aim to reduce environmental impact, from energy-efficient devices to eco-friendly manufacturing practices.

Sustainable Living with Smart Solutions

Smart technologies can contribute to sustainable living. We'll discuss innovations that promote energy conservation, waste reduction, and environmentally conscious practices, creating a greener future.

Learning and Adapting to New Technologies

Lifelong Learning Platforms

As technology evolves, the importance of continuous learning becomes evident. We'll explore lifelong learning platforms that provide seniors with opportunities to acquire new skills, stay informed, and engage in ongoing personal development.

Technology Adoption Support

Adopting new technologies can sometimes be challenging. We'll discuss support systems and resources designed to assist seniors in embracing and confidently using emerging technologies.

The Ethical Considerations of Future Technologies

Ethical Use of Artificial Intelligence

As AI becomes more integrated into daily life, ethical considerations arise. We'll explore the importance of responsible AI development, addressing issues such as bias, privacy, and accountability.

Data Privacy and Security

With increased connectivity comes a need for robust data privacy and security measures. We'll discuss the importance of protecting personal information and understanding the implications of data sharing in the digital age.

Preparing for Tomorrow's Technologies

Staying Informed and Curious

Navigating future technologies involves staying informed and maintaining a curious mindset. We'll discuss strategies for keeping up with technological advancements, exploring new possibilities, and adapting to change.

Community Engagement and Support

Community engagement plays a crucial role in embracing new

technologies. We'll explore how community support, workshops, and shared experiences can foster a sense of technological empowerment among seniors.

The Path Ahead

Embracing Tomorrow with Confidence

As we conclude this chapter, envision the future not as an unknown frontier but as a landscape of opportunities where technology enhances your life. The knowledge gained in this chapter is your key to unlocking the potential of future technologies. In the upcoming chapters, we'll delve into practical tips for staying safe online, discuss the importance of cybersecurity, and take a final optimistic look at the overall journey.

A Technological Tapestry Awaits

Embrace the evolving landscape of technology with open arms, knowing that each advancement is an opportunity for enhanced connection, well-being, and quality of life. The path ahead is filled with exciting possibilities. With the knowledge gained in this chapter, you're ready to embark on a journey of discovery in the ever-expanding world of future technologies.

CHAPTER 13: A DIGITAL SYMPHONY - BRINGING IT ALL TOGETHER

A Holistic Approach to Seniors Embracing Technology

In this chapter, we'll weave together the threads of knowledge from the previous chapters, creating a harmonious symphony that encapsulates the holistic approach to seniors embracing technology. As you journey through the realms of staying connected, understanding the internet, using smartphones, setting up Wi-Fi, engaging in social media, mastering video calls, utilizing cloud services, managing email, working from home, embracing smart home devices, staying safe online, and exploring tomorrow's technology, this chapter serves as the grand finale, offering guidance on integrating these learnings into a cohesive and enriching digital experience.

Reflecting on Your Digital Journey

Celebration of Progress

Before we dive into the integration of technologies, take a moment to reflect on the progress you've made. Celebrate the milestones, both big and small, as you've navigated the digital landscape and embraced various aspects of technology.

Recognizing Growth

Technology adoption is a journey, and growth comes from the willingness to explore, learn, and adapt. Acknowledge your growth in digital literacy, as well as the valuable connections and experiences gained along the way.

Creating Your Digital Blueprint

Personalized Digital Lifestyle

Your digital journey is unique, and so should be your digital blueprint. We'll discuss how to craft a personalized digital lifestyle that aligns with your preferences, interests, and goals, ensuring that technology complements your life rather than overwhelms it.

Prioritizing Your Needs

Identify the aspects of technology that resonate most with your needs. Whether it's staying connected with family, exploring new hobbies online, or utilizing smart home devices for convenience, prioritizing your needs forms the foundation of your digital blueprint.

Seamless Integration of Technologies

Cross-Platform Connectivity

Many technologies discussed in previous chapters can seamlessly integrate for a cohesive experience. We'll explore how cross-platform connectivity can enhance convenience, such as syncing your calendar between your smartphone and smart home devices.

Unified Communication

Integrate communication tools for a unified experience. We'll discuss how email, video calls, and social media can complement each other, creating a comprehensive communication strategy that suits your preferences.

Leveraging Smart Home Synergies

Centralized Smart Home Control

If you've embraced smart home devices, we'll explore how centralizing control through smart home hubs or voice-activated assistants can simplify your interaction with various devices, enhancing the overall smart living experience.

Customizing Smart Home Scenarios

Tailor smart home scenarios to suit different aspects of your life. We'll discuss how you can create custom scenarios for relaxation, productivity, and energy efficiency, ensuring that smart home technologies adapt to your daily rhythms.

Your Digital Sanctuary

Balancing Online and Offline Time

Creating a digital sanctuary involves finding a balance between online and offline activities. We'll discuss strategies for managing screen time, fostering mindfulness, and ensuring that technology enhances your overall well-being.

Curating a Positive Digital Space

Your digital space should be a reflection of positivity. We'll explore how to curate a positive online environment by following uplifting content, engaging in meaningful discussions, and cultivating a digital space that adds value to your life.

Continued Learning and Exploration

Lifelong Learning Opportunities

Technology is ever-evolving, and the journey of learning continues. We'll discuss how to stay engaged with lifelong learning opportunities, exploring new technologies, and adapting to the ongoing advancements in the digital landscape.

Exploring Emerging Technologies

Keep an eye on emerging technologies. We'll provide insights into how to stay informed about upcoming trends, ensuring that you remain at the forefront of technological possibilities and have the knowledge to embrace new innovations.

Fostering a Digital Community

Connecting with Like-Minded Individuals

Digital communities offer opportunities to connect with like-minded individuals. We'll explore online platforms, forums, and groups where you can share experiences, learn from others, and build a supportive digital community.

Engaging in Digital Events

Participate in digital events and activities. We'll discuss virtual events, webinars, and online gatherings that provide opportunities for socializing, learning, and expanding your digital network.

Embracing a Technologically Empowered Lifestyle

The Intersection of Technology and Well-Being

As you bring together various aspects of technology, consider the intersection with your overall well-being. We'll discuss how technology can contribute to physical health, mental well-being, and a sense of fulfillment in your daily life.

Embracing a Digital Symphony

Your journey through the chapters has been a symphony of connections, learning, and empowerment. Embrace the digital symphony that you've created, recognizing the unique melody of your technological journey.

Your Continued Digital Odyssey

Lifelong Exploration

The digital odyssey is lifelong, and your journey doesn't end here. We'll discuss how to approach technology with a sense of curiosity, adaptability, and ongoing exploration, ensuring that you continue to grow and thrive in the digital landscape.

A Future of Possibilities

As you navigate your continued digital journey, envision a future filled with possibilities. The knowledge and experiences gained from this ebook serve as a foundation for embracing the ever-evolving world of technology with confidence and enthusiasm.

CHAPTER 14: A DIGITAL TAPESTRY - NAVIGATING THE SENIOR'S TECHNOLOGY ODYSSEY

Reflecting on the Journey

As we reach the culmination of this ebook, it's time to reflect on the enriching odyssey we've embarked on together. From the introductory call to "Stay Connected" to the optimistic exploration of tomorrow's technologies, each chapter has contributed to weaving a digital tapestry that empowers seniors to navigate the vast landscape of technology with confidence and enthusiasm.

Chapter 1: Introduction to Staying Connected

The journey began with an invitation to recognize the importance of staying connected, emphasizing the profound impact of technology on bridging gaps, fostering relationships, and embracing a vibrant digital life.

Chapters 2-9: Building the Foundation

Chapters 2 to 9 laid the groundwork for a comprehensive understanding of the digital landscape. From unraveling the mysteries of the internet to mastering the art of video calls, the foundation was set for seniors to become adept navigators in the digital sea.

Chapters 10-12: Embracing Technology in Daily Life

Seniors delved into the realm of smart home devices, cybersecurity, and the promises of emerging technologies in chapters 10 to 12. The focus was on transforming living spaces, ensuring online safety, and providing a glimpse into the exciting technological horizons that lie ahead.

Chapter 13: A Digital Symphony - Bringing It All Together

Chapter 13 served as the crescendo, bringing together the threads of knowledge into a harmonious symphony. Seniors were guided on how to seamlessly integrate various technologies, create personalized digital blueprints, and embrace a technologically empowered lifestyle.

A Symphony of Connectivity

The journey celebrated the symphony of connectivity, where seniors learned to utilize smartphones for communication, set up Wi-Fi with ease, socialize on platforms like social media, and engage in seamless video calls. The digital tapestry emphasized that technology is a powerful tool for fostering connections with loved ones and the world at large.

A Symphony of Learning

Seniors embraced the concept of lifelong learning, exploring the intricacies of email communication, cloud services, and even navigating the digital workplace. Each chapter contributed to the melody of continuous growth and adaptation in the ever-evolving technological landscape.

A Symphony of Safety

Safety was paramount in the symphony, as seniors learned the essentials of staying safe online, recognizing and avoiding cyber threats, and adopting ethical practices in the digital realm. The harmony of online safety resonated through every interaction, ensuring a secure and empowering digital experience.

A Symphony of Well-Being

The digital tapestry prioritized well-being, acknowledging the importance of balancing online and offline time, creating positive digital spaces, and leveraging technology for both physical and mental health. Seniors were encouraged to curate a digital sanctuary that contributes to overall well-being.

The Final Movement: A Digital Odyssey

As we conclude this ebook, envision the collective knowledge and experiences gained as a guide for a continued digital odyssey.

The journey doesn't end here; rather, it serves as a prelude to a future filled with possibilities, continuous exploration, and a technologically empowered lifestyle.

The Digital Tapestry Continues

The digital tapestry woven through this ebook is a testament to the resilience, adaptability, and enthusiasm of seniors in embracing technology. The final movement is an invitation to continue this tapestry, exploring new technologies, staying connected with communities, and contributing to the ongoing symphony of digital empowerment.

Your Digital Journey Unfurls

As the final notes of this digital symphony resonate, consider the landscape of possibilities that technology unfolds for you. Your digital journey is unique, marked by growth, connections, and the continuous pursuit of knowledge. The path ahead is filled with exciting opportunities, and your digital tapestry is a reflection of the vibrant melody you've created in the digital realm.

Embrace the Future

Embrace the future with open arms, knowing that you possess the knowledge, skills, and resilience to navigate the ever-evolving technological landscape. The final movement is not an end but a new beginning, where the digital tapestry you've woven continues to unfold, creating a legacy of empowerment and enthusiasm for generations to come.